21.-

12/07

FLIES

by Sophie Lockwood

Content Adviser: Michael Breed, Ph.D., Professor,
Ecology and Evolutionary Biology,
The University of Colorado, Boulder

THE CHILD'S WORLD®, MANKATO, MINNESOTA

Flies

Published in the United States of America by The Child's World®
1980 Lookout Drive • Mankato, MN 56003-1705
800-599-READ • www.childsworld.com

Acknowledgements:

The Child's World®: Mary Berendes, Publishing Director

The Creative Spark: Mary Francis, Project Director; Wendy Mead, Editor; Deborah Goodsite, Photo Researcher

The Design Lab: Kathleen Petelinsek, Designer and Production Artist

Photos:

Cover and title page: Andrei Scarf/Dreamstime.com; frontispiece and CIP: Glenn Young/Bigstockphoto.com

Interior: Alamy: 8 (Phototake Inc.), 22 (blickwinkel); Animals Animals: 5, 9 (Bernard Photo Productions); AP Photo: 30 (Gareth Morgan); Corbis: 37 (Robert Patrick/Sygma); iStockphoto.com: 5, 13, 14, 33 (Arlindo Silva), 5, 27, 34 (David Acosta Allely); Minden Pictures: 21 (Kim Taylor/npl), 25 (Stephen Dalton); Oxford Scientific: 16, (Oxford Scientific), 29 (Raymond Mendez); Photo Researchers, Inc.: 7 (USDA/Nature Source), 5, 19 (Dirk Wiersma); Visuals Unlimited: 5, 11 (Dr. Stanley Flegler).

Library of Congress Cataloging-in-Publication Data

Lockwood, Sophie.
  Flies / by Sophie Lockwood.
      p. cm.—(The world of insects)
  Includes index.
  ISBN-13: 978-1-59296-822-0 (library bound: alk. paper)
  ISBN-10: 1-59296-822-8 (library bound: alk. paper)
  1. Flies—Juvenile literature. I. Title. II. Series.
  QL533.2.L63 2007
  595.77—dc22   2007000182

TABLE OF CONTENTS

⊕

Chapter One

A Fly on Your Banana

The bananas have been on the counter for several days, and now tiny flies are buzzing around them. These are fruit flies, sometimes called vinegar flies, and they are so annoying. Or are they?

These pesky insects may well unlock the key to curing some serious human diseases. Fruit flies may help scientists discover ways to prevent diseases carried in our **genes**, such as cancer and Alzheimer's disease. They might help us solve the puzzle of such **genetic** diseases as cystic fibrosis, sickle cell anemia, or Tay-Sachs. Can we truly expect all this from a fruit fly? Yes!

Vinegar flies, officially called *Drosophila melanogaster,* measure about 3 millimeters (0.125 inches) long. Normally, this species is attracted to overripe fruit, on which it lays eggs that quickly hatch to become **larvae**. The entire life cycle of a fruit fly lasts from 8 to 15 days.

For the past 100 years, scientists have studied fruit flies to determine how

Did You Know?
In the Middle Ages, people believed that maggots (fly larvae) came from rotting meat. They did not realize the maggots were flies in the making.

Fruit flies can be found all around the world.

an animal's genetic material is coded to determine its physical traits. Because the vinegar fly's life cycle is short, it takes little time to see if a physical trait is passed on from parent to offspring.

In 2000, the vinegar fly became the largest animal to have its DNA completely mapped. Mapping DNA is determining the genetic factors that affect an animal's body. By understanding how DNA works, scientists expect to be able to figure out how genetic diseases are carried on genes and how genetic problems can be fixed.

Would You Believe?
Female fruit flies can lay up to 2,000 eggs—a remarkable quantity of eggs for an insect that's only 3 to 4 millimeters (0.12 to 0.16 inches) long.

Scientists study flies to learn more about genetics.

While thousands of fruit flies breed in labs throughout the world, their close cousins thrive in many diverse habitats. They live in homes, in restaurants, and at fruit and vegetable markets. Any garbage dump where rotting fruits or vegetables, juice bottles, or even used ketchup packets can be found provides an ideal breeding ground for fruit flies. These insects love to eat the yeast growing in rotting fruit or juice. Next time there is a fly on your banana, think about what that species is doing for human beings before you swat!

Fruit flies can be found almost everywhere.

Chapter Two

The Fly Cycle of Life

Everyone knows what a fly looks like. Flies are the insects that buzz around our picnics. They swarm over animal dung in the backyard or rotting animal carcasses on the side of the road.

Flies, like other insects, have six legs and three body parts: head, **thorax**, and **abdomen**. What makes flies interesting is the number of species there are and their unusual physical features. Flies are not the most diverse insect order—beetles actually have the greatest number of species. However, within the 120,000 species of flies, there are a wide range of sizes, body styles, habitats, and feeding habits.

Many insects bear the name "fly," but they are not true flies. Butterflies and dragonflies are obviously not true flies, but neither are mayflies, caddis flies, sawflies, or scorpion flies. True flies belong to the family Diptera, whose name comes from the Greek words for "two wings." It is those wings that, in part, make flies special.

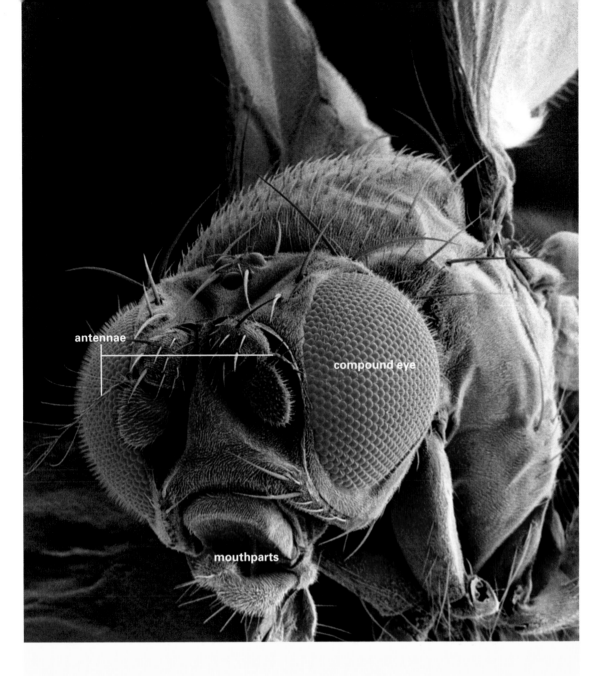

antennae

compound eye

mouthparts

BODY PARTS

A fly's head has **antennae**, mouthparts, and compound eyes. The antennae have three basic segments and allow the

This close-up photograph shows the head of a fruit fly.

fly to smell. Mouthparts include mandibles, or jaws, and a system for sucking, lapping, and sponging up liquids. Most flies drink their meals and rely on a pumping system in their heads to suck in fruit juices, body fluids, or blood.

A fly's eyes are compound eyes, called **ommatidia**. The eyes are large, taking up much of the head, and many flies can see almost 360 degrees. When humans approach flies from behind, they are not sneaking up on the flies—they can see people coming.

The thorax of a fly is the central section of the body and houses the fly's wings, muscles, and legs. A fly has a very different set of wings from most insects. Dragonflies, butterflies, and beetles have two pairs of wings. True flies have one pair of working wings that are similar to other insects' wings. The second pair are stunted, nonfunctioning nubs called **halteres**, located where the second pair of wings used to be. Halteres provide balance during flight.

The average fly flaps its wings 200 times a second. Not every flap is produced by muscle power. Flies have the ability to force their wings up and down by moving the thorax. This motion can be compared to tightening and releasing a spring. The thorax contracts and releases the wings, which bounce up and down

Did You Know?
Flies have no eyelids. To keep their eyes clean, they wipe them regularly with the hairs on their legs.

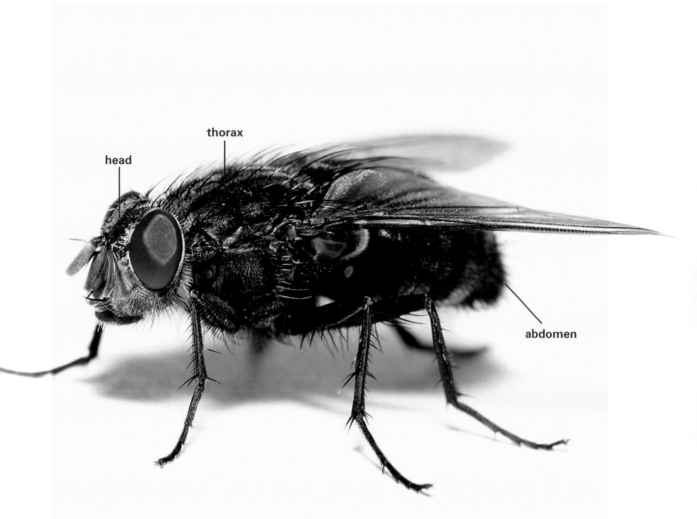

head

thorax

abdomen

rapidly, like a compressed spring would when released. This saves energy and allows flies to move quickly.

Flies breathe through tiny holes in their bodies called **spiracles**. Oxygen enters the body through the holes

A fly's body has three main sections: head, thorax, and abdomen.

and is used, and waste gas leaves the body through the same holes. Unlike humans, flies do not have blood. They

Flies, such as this blue fly, have hemolymph instead of blood.

have a greenish fluid called **hemolymph** that flows through the body and carries nutrients from their food. Oxygen is not carried in hemolymph.

A fly's abdomen contains its digestive and reproductive organs. The digestive system is basically a long tube. As the fly takes in liquid, the nutrients are taken out of the fluid and used in the body. The waste is eliminated from the body through the anus at the base of the abdomen.

Female flies produce eggs that must be fertilized by males to produce young. The females lay their eggs on a food source, possibly rotting fruit or decaying flesh. Their sense of smell is very acute. The flies can locate food several kilometers away and head to the food source to lay their eggs. Flies are not caring mothers. They lay their eggs and leave.

LIFE CYCLE

Female flies may lay from one egg up to 2,000 eggs. The number of eggs produced depends on the species and the conditions. The life cycle of a fly is an example of complete **metamorphosis**. The fly goes through four stages of life: egg, larva (maggot), **pupa**, and adult. This is the same process a butterfly goes through, but flies become adults more quickly and less dramatically.

Depending on the species, the eggs hatch after one to several days. In some cases, the eggs survive over the winter

A housefly larva must eat a lot to survive.

and hatch in the spring. The wormlike critters that emerge are the larvae, also called maggots. A maggot's primary job is to eat and grow. A maggot goes through several growth stages called instars. The length of each of these stages depends on several factors, including food availability, temperature, and weather conditions.

During the pupa stage, the maggot changes its body shape inside a puparium. The protective puparium is a hard shell, usually rusty brown in color. When the adult fly is ready to emerge, it breaks through the puparium. The pupa stage can last days or weeks, depending on the species.

Most flies do not live a full year. Tiny fruit flies may have a life span as short as a week or two, while their larger relatives may survive for several months. Many species of true flies spend most of their lives as maggots or pupae. The egg stage and the adult stage are generally short.

Once a fly becomes an adult, its main goal is to mate and produce young. Flies, like many bird species, dance to entice their mates. The better the dance, the greater chance a male has of winning a female.

PREDATORS

A chameleon sits motionless on branch in a Madagascaran rain forest. A small fly hovers over a flower and ZAP! The chameleon's tongue darts out and makes a meal of the fly. MMMMM, tasty!

Flies do not appear on the menu of every animal in the jungle, but most **insectivores** are happy to eat both maggots and adult flies. Because maggots group together and are easy to catch, predators can eat an entire meal at one time. Most bats eat true flies, although they might prefer mosquitoes. Lizards, toads, newts, and frogs happily feed on flies or maggots. Some birds bear the name flycatcher because of their main food source—flies. Spiders catch flies in their webs and store the bodies for a later feast. Ground beetles, rodents, shrews, and moles usually eat fly larvae or pupae.

Flies also need to heed the plants on which they land. The Venus flytrap comes by its name naturally—this plant, native to North and South Carolina, lures flies in, snaps shut, and slowly digests its victims. Other fly-eating plants include sundews and bladderworts.

Chapter Three

Flies, Flies, and More Flies

About 225 million years ago, huge dinosaurs grazed on the ample plants living on Earth. Early mammals appeared, and turtles and crocodiles sunned themselves near lakes and rivers. These creatures and others produced massive amounts of dung, the ideal habitat for breeding true flies. It was during this period that true

This ancient fly was found preserved in amber.

flies first appeared, and they have buzzed and bitten their way through history ever since.

Early flies were caught between layers of rock and in oozing pine sap. We find them as fossils encased in sandstone or amber. There are 3,125 species of flies known only from fossils, including the oldest, a limoniid crane fly. Today, 120,000 fly species live in every ecosystem in the world, except in the coldest polar regions.

Some of these flies live remarkable lives. Phantom midge larvae are transparent and use air bubbles in their bodies to float in water. These larvae have large jaws that they use to catch water fleas. Some flies mine holes in leaves, producing tunnels that create unique patterns. Other fly larvae prefer the taste of snail to any other food. They devour the nonessential parts of the snail before eating the vital parts, so they can have fresh meat longer.

Flies have only one defense—flight. They escape from predators by flying, and some fly very quickly. Midges beat their wings 62,760 beats per minute. A tabanid fly, related to the horsefly, has been clocked at 145 kilometers per hour (90 miles per hour). Tabanid flies have unusual green eyes with orange and yellow stripes that look much like trendy sunglasses.

Did You Know?
There are no giants in the world of true flies. The largest true flies measure about 30 millimeters (1.18 inches) long. These include robber flies, Japanese *shioya abu*, and crane flies.

SUBORDERS OF FLIES

With so many species, true flies cover a wide range of sizes, shapes, colors, and habitats. The easiest way to group flies is by suborder: Nematocera (NEM-eh-TAHS-uh-ruh), Brachycera (bra-KY-suh-ruh), and Cyclorrhapha (sy-KLOR-uh-fuh).

Did You Know?
Tiny midges and no-see-ums measure about 1 millimeter (0.04 inch) long—but they pack a mean bite.

A hoverfly caught doing what it does best—hovering!

Nematocera, a term that means "threadlike antennae," includes both large and small flies. Most flies in this family are tiny—midges, punkies, and no-see-ums. The largest, crane flies, look much like mosquitoes. In fact, mosquitoes are a family within this suborder. About 2,000 species in this family are water midges, tiny flies that swarm around ponds and streams in early summer.

A tiny member of Nematocera bites a human.

Punkies and No-see-ums

What kinds of insects have such silly names as punkies and no-see-ums? Well, these are common names for types of true flies, and they are very small. They also bite. You won't see them, but you'll know when they've bitten you.

No-see-ums and punkies are very small, biting midges, roughly 1 to 3 millimeters (0.04 to 0.11 inches) long. There are more than 4,000 species of these minute critters, and they are most common in coastal regions, particularly at dawn and dusk. Like mosquitoes, only the females drink blood. Once mated, a female needs a blood meal in order to lay her eggs. Depending on the species and the size of the meal, the female may lay from 20 to 150 eggs.

The larvae need moisture to survive. They prefer salt marshes and mangrove swamps, tropical areas with rotting fruit or wood, springs, or streams.

Brachycera (short-horned flies) contains about 120 families and covers an assortment of flies with short antennae. This diverse suborder includes robber flies, bee flies, snipe flies, window flies, horseflies, and humpback flies. These are large flies, and some are quite aggressive. Robber flies attack other flies, dragonflies, wasps, bees, and even spiders. Humpback flies attach themselves to spiders and live their lives on their hosts.

Cyclorrhapha are the flies most of us know best—houseflies. Other flies in this suborder include hoverflies or flower flies, phorid or coffin flies, dung flies, and fruit flies. Phorid flies are used as biological controls for fire ants. Adult phorid flies lay their eggs on fire ant workers, and their larvae eat the ants alive. Hoverflies are bright yellow and black, and are often mistaken for small bees or wasps. Blowflies or flesh flies bite through the flesh of dead animals. Some will feed on living flesh, and their larvae will even feed on the tough hides of elephants or rhinos. Louse flies are blood feeders that prey on mammals and birds. One species feeds only on bats, and their larvae live in caves occupied by great colonies of bats.

Did You Know?
Human botflies, found only in Central and South America, lay tiny eggs in a mosquito. When the mosquito bites a human, the botfly eggs are transferred to the human, entering the skin through the mosquito bite. The larvae feed on human flesh and emerge through the skin as adults.

Most of the flies we see every day are from the Cyclorrhapha suborder.

Chapter Four

In Appreciation of Flies

The *Book of Nature,* an old, sacred text, tells how bees and flies came to be the way they are. Like many myths, this one may not have the facts straight, but the characteristics of bees and flies it describes are true enough:

> Two tribes of little people lived near each other. One of the tribes looked for food each day and stored it safely for winter. The other tribe spent its days playing in the sun.
>
> "Come and play with us," said the lazy ones.
>
> The busy workers answered, "No, come and work with us. Winter is coming, and we need food for the cold days ahead."

The busy people brought honey from the flowers, while the lazy people danced and sang. The lazy ones thought, "Those busy workers will have enough food stored for two tribes, and we shall eat well. Let us play some more."

When winter came, the busy workers felt sorry for their neighbors. "We will give them some honey." The lazy ones enjoyed the efforts of those who had worked, and both survived.

Flies are a part of many myths and legends.

The following summer, the workers said, "It would be easier to store food if we lived closer to the meadow." So the workers walked away, but the lazy ones did not worry. They were positive their friends would return and feed them again through the winter.

Winter came again. The workers ate well, while the lazy people starved. The Great Spirit said, "Busy workers, I will give you wings, and you shall be bees. You will not have to walk from flower to flower to collect honey. Humans will admire you for your hard work."

To the lazy ones, the Great Spirit said, "You shall be flies, and you, too, shall have wings. While the bees eat honey, you shall have only rubbish. When humans see you, they will drive you away."

There are many fables, legends, and folktales that tell about flies. Few are very complimentary, because humans have associated flies with decay and dung for centuries.

If anything, people have worked hard to find ways to avoid or repel flies. They have tried using clumps of lion fat, wolf

tails, and sticky traps, like flypaper. Useful flyswatters have ranged from the natural (tails of animals or palm fronds) to the manufactured plastic versions, to whatever is close at hand—a rolled-up newspaper or a shoe.

Humans have found many ways to get rid of flies.

MEDICAL MIRACLES

Few people see flies as anything but annoying, dirty creatures that should be sprayed, swatted, or otherwise eliminated. However, there are some doctors and patients who are thankful that flies and their larvae exist.

A scientist examines some maggots, which are used to treat some kinds of wounds.

Maggots—fly larvae—are remarkably helpful in cleaning wounds by getting rid of dead tissue. They disinfect wounds by killing bacteria, and they encourage healthy flesh to grow. This is no joke! And it is not some kind of torture from the Middle Ages.

In 2003, the U.S. Food and Drug Administration approved two medical devices for use on patients—maggots and leeches. Maggots are the larvae of flies, and leeches are blood-sucking worms. Many patients who were at risk of losing limbs because of serious infections credit maggots for their recovery.

Here is a true story of successful maggot therapy: In 2003, Pam Mitchell got a small cut on her foot that became infected. The affected area was removed surgically, but the infection continued to spread. Antibiotics simply did not work, and doctors recommended amputating her foot. Desperate, Mitchell found a doctor willing to try maggot therapy. After ten treatments, her foot was nearly healed, the skin looked healthy, and Mitchell was sold on maggots.

Maggot therapy works on infections, wounds, and burned skin. The maggots used are not scooped out of garbage cans. They are grown in laboratories and supplied to hospitals for use. More than 300 hospitals in the United States rely on blowfly maggots to help cure certain patients.

Chapter Five

Man and Flies

What would the world be like without flies? Some people might think the extinction of all flies would be a good thing. They should think again. Flies play an active role in the balance of nature. They, like every other creature, have both positive and negative effects on the environments in which they live.

Flies are among the most common insects that are known to visit flowers. They pollinate 555 species of flowers and 100 types of cultivated plants. Next to bees and wasps, flies are responsible for pollinating the most flowers.

True fly larvae make excellent biological control agents. Hoverfly or flower fly maggots devour aphids, mealybugs, and scale insects, all of which damage plants. Many female hoverflies look for colonies of aphids when laying their eggs. These maggots are a gardener's delight, eliminating plant pests. Larvae of gall midges eat spider mites, thrips, and whiteflies, as well as aphids. Gall midges are often

purchased as a pest-control device for organic apple orchards. The larvae of marsh flies feed on snails and slugs along the banks of ponds and streams.

Adult flies can also be active predators. Long-legged flies feed on small insects that live around ponds. Robber flies prey on wasps, bees, dragonflies, grasshoppers, and whatever other insects come into their areas. Friendly flies, a slower, larger relative of houseflies, help control tent caterpillars in forests. The flies deposit live maggots into the cocoons. The maggots feed on the caterpillars and then drop to the forest floor to pupate over the winter.

Hoverflies feed on plant nectar and pollen.

AN ONGOING WAR

In some countries, flies are more annoying than dangerous. Australia is one such place. The increase in the fly population came about because of changes made to the Australian landscape by humans. In a normal natural environment, there are checks and balances that

Flies, such as this killer fly, can reproduce quickly and sometimes overwhelm an environment.

keep population growth under control. In Australia, the introduction of cattle and sheep threw that balance off kilter.

Cattle and sheep produce massive amounts of dung, and dung is just what bushflies need for breeding. Australian scientists looked for a way to reduce the fly population and turned to the dung beetle. In actual fact, they turned to dozens of species of dung beetles. These beetles "processed" dung so quickly that fly populations began to decrease. In 1998, increased dung beetle activity reduced fly populations to 97 percent mortality—fewer flies were produced than died.

Scientists have to determine just the right time to introduce dung beetles into an environment. Not all introductions are completely successful and at times, a surge in the dung beetle population needs to be controlled, too.

DEADLY DISEASES

While maggots return flesh to good health in hospitals and laboratories, their adult relatives carry diseases that, at the least, make people sick and, at the worst, kill them. Among the most well-known disease carriers of the fly world are sand flies, horseflies, biting midges, blackflies, houseflies, and tsetse flies.

Common houseflies can carry up to 100 disease-causing agents, from bacteria and viruses to **parasites**. The flies do not need to bite humans to make them sick. They can deposit the disease agents on food with their leg hairs or by tasting the food. Serious diseases carried by houseflies include cholera, typhoid fever, dysentery (extreme diarrhea), and anthrax.

Blood-sucking flies, such as midges, sand flies, horse-flies, and punkies, can carry viruses and small worms that are parasites. Loiasis, a human disease caused by tiny worms, affects joints and muscles and can cause skin rashes. Blackflies, although they do not carry disease to humans in the United States, do cause serious problems in Africa. Common along rivers, blackflies pass on tiny worms that attack the eyes and lead to blindness or vision problems. The World Health Organization estimates that 17.7 million people have contracted this parasite, and 270,000 of those have gone blind.

Leishmaniasis, one of the least known but most serious infectious diseases in the world, can be spread by infected sand flies to humans through bites. This disease is rarely heard of in the United States but is common in the Middle East. African tsetse flies also

Would You Believe?
The next time a fly tiptoes over your outdoor barbecue, think about this: Scientists think houseflies carry around 1,941,000 different kinds of bacteria. Which ones do you want to eat with your supper?

carry parasites that lead to a condition called sleeping sickness. Sleeping sickness is a death sentence. In Africa, the number of cases of sleeping sickness has risen by 15 percent in recent years, with between 250,000 and 300,000 people dying from the disease each year.

Both friend and foe, flies fulfill a needed role in nature. They rid us of some pests and provide food for other, larger animals. They groom gardens and pollinate flowers. They also carry diseases and become an annoyance both at home and outdoors. They make pretty good subjects for science fiction movies, too.

Tsetse flies, such as this one, can carry parasites.

Glossary

abdomen (AB-doh-men) the elongated portion of the body of an arthropod, located behind the thorax

antennae (an-TEN-nee) thin, sensory organs found on the heads of many insects

genes (JEENZ) the basic units of information able to transmit characteristics, such as eye color or height, from one generation to the next

genetic (jeh-NET-ik) involving or resulting from genes

halteres (HALL-teerz) small, nubbed structures that help flies balance during flight

hemolymph (HEE-moh-lymf) a bloodlike fluid in the bodies of many invertebrates

insectivores (in-SEHK-tih-vohrz) animals that eat insects as their main food source

larva (LAHR-vuh) wormlike life stage of insects that develop into the pupa stage; the plural is *larvae* (LAHR-vee)

metamorphosis (meht-uh-MOR-foh-sis) a complete change in body form as an animal becomes an adult

ommatidia (ahm-uh-TIH-dee-uh) the visual facets of an insect eye

parasites (PAH-ruh-sightz) plants or animals that live on or in another host organism

pupa (PYOO-puh) the insect stage during which an immature larva develops into an adult; the plural is *pupae* (PYOO-pee)

spiracles (SPEER-uh-kulz) small openings in the side of an insect, used for breathing

thorax (THOR-aks) the middle section of an insect, crustacean, or spider

For More Information

Watch It

Bug City: Flies and Mosquitoes, VHS. (Wynnewood, PA: Schlessinger Media, 1998.)

Insectia 2, DVD. (Montreal: Pixcom, 2005.)

Really Gross Bug Stuff, VHS. (Wynnewood, PA: Schlessinger Media, 1998.)

Secret of Life On Earth, DVD. (New York: IMAX, 2002.)

Read It

Brimmer, Larry Dane. *Flies*. Danbury, CT: Children's Press, 2000.

Camper, Cathy. *Bugs Before Time: Prehistoric Insects and Their Relatives*. New York: Simon & Schuster Children's Publishing, 2002.

Jackson, Donna M. *The Bug Scientists*. Boston: Houghton Mifflin, 2004.

McEvey, Shane. *Flies*. Broomall, PA: Chelsea House, 2001.

Merrick, Patrick. *Biting Flies*. Chanhassen, MN: The Child's World, 2000.

Woodward, John. *The Secret World of Flies*. Chicago: Raintree, 2003.

Look It Up

Visit our Web site for lots of links about flies:
http://www.childsworld.com/links

Note to Parents, Teachers, and Librarians: We routinely verify our Web links to make sure they are safe, active sites—so encourage your readers to check them out!

The Animal Kingdom
Where Do Flies Fit In?

Kingdom: Animalia

Phylum: Arthropoda

Class: Insecta

Order: Diptera

Species: 120,000 species

Relatives: Gnats and mosquitoes

Index

About the Author
Sophie Lockwood is a former teacher and a longtime writer. She writes textbooks, newspaper articles, and magazine articles. Sophie enjoys writing about animals and their habits. The most interesting part of her research, Sophie says, is learning how scientists apply their knowledge to save endangered species. She lives with her husband in the foothills of the Blue Ridge Mountains.